MW01222529

THINGS THAT GO
WORKBOOK

For Preschoolers

Written by Martha Cheney
Illustrated by Karol Kaminski

LOWELL HOUSE JUVENILE

LOS ANGELES

NTC/Contemporary Publishing Group

*Reviewed and endorsed by Andrea Penn-Kraus, M.Ed.,
private tutor and former elementary teacher*

Published by Lowell House
A division of NTC/Contemporary Publishing Group, Inc.
4255 West Touhy Avenue, Lincolnwood (Chicago), Illinois 60712 U.S.A.

Managing Director and Publisher: Jack Artenstein
Director of Publishing Services: Rena Copperman
Editorial Director: Brenda Pope-Ostrow
Director of Art Production: Bret Perry
Editor: Linda Gorman
Typesetter: Carolyn Wendt
Color Artist: Lynn Haaland

Lowell House books can be purchased at special discounts when ordered in bulk
for premiums and special sales. Please contact Customer Service at:
NTC/Contemporary Publishing Group
4255 W. Touhy Avenue
Lincolnwood, IL 60712
1-800-323-4900

Printed in Hong Kong by Imago

ISBN: 0-7373-0340-9

10 9 8 7 6 5 4 3 2 1

BOOKS will help develop your child's natural talents hance critical and creative thinking skills. These skills how to think. They are precisely the skills emphasized ldren.

INGS THAT GO WORKBOOK FOR
en's critical and creative thinking skills while teaching move on land, over and under water, through the sky, ivities introduce children to cars, trucks, trains, boats, Higher-level thinking skills promoted throughout ionships, visual discrimination, and creative thinking. icate the specific thinking skills developed on that page.

OOK also combines full-color art with black-and- oung children's learning and creativity. The full-color identify colors, while the black-and-white pages reative imaginations to draw or color pictures.

n range from easier to more difficult. Read the em. Let your child choose to do the activities that es, stop. A page or two at a time may be enough, as ng.

BOOKS have been written and endorsed by educators. demonstrates curiosity, imagination, a sense of fun and o learn. These books will open your child's mind to her true potential.

THINGS THAT GO

It is a busy day in the city. Everyone has somewhere to go!
Name the things people are riding in or riding on.
Name the places people are going.

Things that carry people and objects from place to place are called **vehicles**.

How many different kinds of vehicles can you find in the picture?

Which vehicle has the most wheels?

Find some things in the picture that are orange. Can you name them?

CARS

Cars take us where we want to go. Some cars are small and some cars are big. Some are new and some are old.
Color the smallest car blue.
Color the biggest car red.
Color the rest of the cars any way you like.

Draw a circle around the car you like best.
Which car is old? How can you tell?

A FAMILY CAR

Draw a picture of your family's car in the space below.
If your family does not have a car, draw a picture of a car
you would like to have.

Where would you like to go in the car?
Who would you take with you?

A CITY BUS

How many people are inside the bus?
How many people are waiting in line to get on the bus?
Who is the oldest person in the picture? How do you know?

Find two objects that are shaped like a circle.
Find two objects that are shaped like a square.
Find two objects that are shaped like a triangle.
Tell a story about the picture.

TRUCKS

Trucks carry all kinds of things that people need.
What do these trucks carry? In the boxes, draw a picture of
something you might find in each truck.

What are some other things that trucks carry?

MOTORCYCLES

Motorcycles are vehicles that have two wheels. Sometimes police officers ride motorcycles. They always wear helmets for protection.

Look at the motorcycles below. Two of them are exactly alike. Can you find the two matching motorcycles?

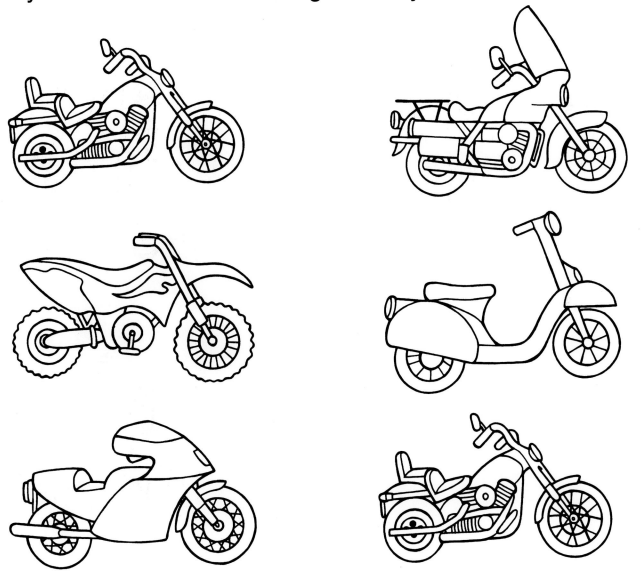

Color the matching motorcycles your favorite color. Color the rest of the motorcycles any way you like.

AIRPLANES

Airplanes are vehicles that fly. They take off and land at an airport. Some airplanes carry many passengers. Other airplanes can carry only one or two people.
Find the gray airplane. Find the yellow airplane. Which airplane is bigger?

How is an airplane like a bird? How is it different?
Have you ever ridden in an airplane? Where did you go?

HELICOPTERS

Helicopters can fly, too. They can go straight up in the air. They can stay in one place in the air. They can land in a small space.

Say the word **helicopter**. What sound does it begin with? What other objects in the picture begin with the same sound?

SPACE SHUTTLE

A space shuttle is a special kind of flying vehicle. It can go into space! A space shuttle can't take off by itself. It is launched into space on a rocket.

How many triangle shapes can you find in the picture?

How many circle shapes can you find?

How many rectangle shapes can you find?

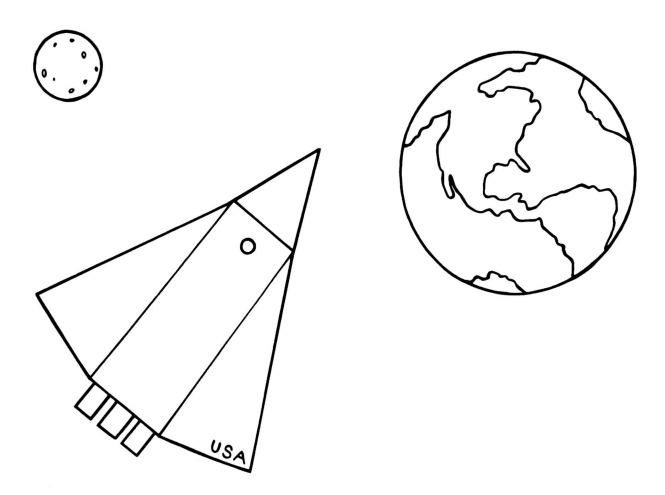

Would you like to go into space? Why or why not?

A NEW WAY TO FLY

Draw a vehicle for this pilot to fly.
Use your imagination. Try to create
a new kind of flying machine.

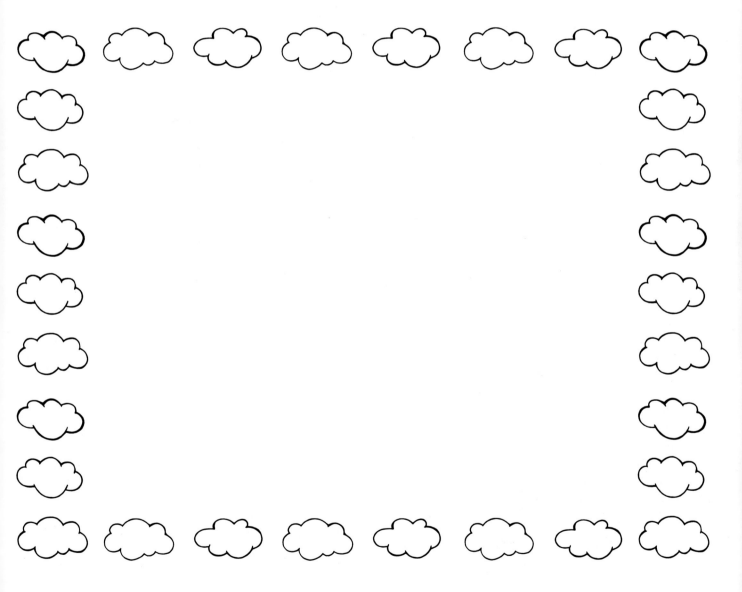

What will you call your new vehicle?

HOT-AIR BALLOONS

People fly in hot-air balloons mostly for fun. Hot-air balloons are used for sight-seeing and sometimes for racing.

Tina is riding in one of the hot-air balloons below. Use the clues to find Tina.

    Tina is not riding in the smallest balloon.

    She is not riding in the blue balloon.

Where is Tina? What color is her balloon?

A BLIMP

This is a blimp. It is very, very big. People ride in the little compartment on the bottom of the blimp. Blimps are often used to take pictures from the air.

Look at the shadows on the ground. Which shadow is made by the blimp? What do you think are making the other shadows?

Do you think a blimp flies fast or slow? Why?

BUNCHES OF BOATS

Boats travel on water. Big ships carry cargo and people across the ocean. Motorboats pull water-skiers. These boats have engines to make them go.

Sailboats skim over the waves. Sailboats use the power of the wind to make them go.

How many sailboats do you see in this picture?

How many boats are there all together?

Color the smallest sailboat purple.
Color the biggest ship blue.
Color one motorboat red and one yellow.
Color the rest of the picture any way you like.
Have you ever been on a boat? Where did you go?

A ROWBOAT

A rowboat doesn't have a motor. It takes muscle power to make a rowboat go!
Wesley is using oars to move the rowboat through the water. Jasmine is in the rowboat, too.

What is Jasmine doing?
Where do you think Wesley and Jasmine are going?
Tell a story about the picture.

A FERRY BOAT

A ferry boat takes the place of a bridge. It carries cars and people across a river or a bay.
How many people are riding on the ferry?
How many cars are on the ferry?

TUGBOATS

Tugboats are small but mighty. They are used to pull big, flat boats called barges up a river. Barges are loaded with cargo such as coal, steel, or lumber.

Find tugboat number 1. Color it green.
Find tugboat number 2. Color it gray.
Find tugboat number 3. Color it brown.
Color the rest of the picture any way you like.

A GONDOLA

This unusual boat is called a gondola. If you want to ride in a gondola, you should go to Venice, Italy. In Venice, the gondola is used as a taxi on the canals that run through the city.

Look at the pattern of shapes on the side of the gondola.
Color each square in the pattern purple.
Color each triangle yellow.
Color each circle green.
What should the next shape in the pattern be?

A SUBMARINE

A submarine is a special kind of boat that goes under the water.

If you were riding in a submarine, what kinds of things do you think you might see from the window? Look at the picture for clues.

Say the word **submarine**. What sound does it begin with?
What other objects in the picture begin with the same sound?
Which animal is as big as the submarine?
Which animal has lots of arms?

ON THE FARM

Some vehicles are made to do work on a farm. A tractor does many jobs. What is the tractor doing in this picture?
Name all the farm animals you see in the picture.
What sound does each animal make?
What other animals might be found on a farm?

Color the barn red.
Color the pig pink.
Color the hay yellow.
Color the rest of the picture any way you like.
What season does this picture show? How can you tell?

A TRAIN

A train is a huge, powerful vehicle. It has special wheels that can run only on tracks.

Here is a poem about a train. Learn the words and then say the poem for someone in your family.

Big train rolling down the track
Will you soon be coming back?
I would like to ride along
And listen to your choo-choo song.

Where do you think the train might be going?

PARTS OF A TRAIN

This part of a train is called the locomotive. The locomotive has a powerful engine.

This is a box car. It looks like a big box. It carries cargo such as furniture.

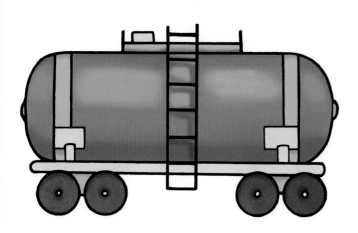

This is a tanker car. It carries liquids such as milk.

This is the caboose. The caboose is the last car on the train.

Which part of the train pulls the other cars?
What other cargo could the box car carry?
What other liquids could the tanker car carry?

A SUBWAY

A subway is a special kind of train that runs on tracks in a tunnel under the ground.

Josie, Janet, and their mother are waiting for the subway to pull into the station.

Josie loves to ride on the subway. Draw a circle around her.

Janet doesn't like to ride on the subway. Draw a square around her.

Why do you think Josie and Janet's mother is holding their hands?

TROLLEYS

A trolley, or streetcar, is another vehicle that runs on tracks.
The trolley's tracks are on the street. If you visit the city of
San Francisco, California, you can ride on a trolley.
Which trolley is going up a hill?
Which trolley is going down a hill?
How do you know?

How many people are riding the trolleys all together?

THINGS THAT GO ON ICE AND SNOW

In some parts of the world, snow and ice cover the ground much of the time. The people who live in these wintry places have special ways to go over the ice and snow.

Describe the different things people are doing in the picture.

Are more people skiing or skating?
How many dogs are pulling the dogsled?
What special clothes are people wearing to keep warm?
Which activity would you like to do most? Why?

FUN IN THE SUN

Many people like to play and work outside.
What are the people in the park doing?
Why are the children wearing helmets?

Find something that goes on two wheels and is fun to ride. Color it blue.

Find something that goes when you push it. Color it red.

Color the sky to show that it is a bright, sunny day.

Color the rest of the picture any way you like.

UNICYCLES

These clowns are riding unicycles. A unicycle has just one wheel! Do you think it would be hard or easy to ride a unicycle?

There are five things hidden in this picture. Can you find a flower, a jump rope, a kite, a doll, and a drum?

A VAN

This is a van. A van is used to carry people or cargo.
Say the word **van**. What sound does it begin with?
Name the items inside the van. They all begin with the
same sound.

There are two items outside the van. Which one of them
starts with the same sound as **van**?
Which object makes music?
Which object can you wear?

WHAT DO THEY DO?

Here are two vehicles that have very special jobs.
Which vehicle is used to carry sick people to the hospital?
Color it red.
Which vehicle is used in a race? Color it yellow.

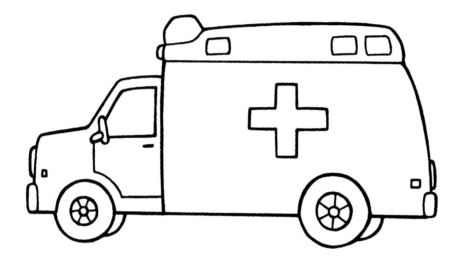

Which vehicle has a siren?
Do these vehicles go fast or slow? Why?

WHAT'S WRONG WITH THIS PICTURE?

Something is wrong with this bus!
Draw the missing parts of the bus.
Draw three happy children in the bus.

What kind of bus is this?
What color should it be?

VEHICLE MATCHING

Match each vehicle to the person who might use it.

What is each vehicle called?
Which vehicle does not go on land?

MORE MATCHING

Match each vehicle to the person who might use it.

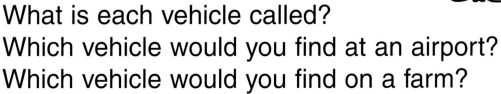

What is each vehicle called?
Which vehicle would you find at an airport?
Which vehicle would you find on a farm?

FAST AND SLOW

Look at the vehicles on these two pages.
Find something that flies and goes fast. Color it blue.
Find something that rolls on wheels and goes fast. Color it purple.

Find something that moves on the water and goes fast.
Color it green.
Find something that goes slow. Color it yellow.
Color the rest of the picture any way you like.
Tell a story about the picture.

WHAT DOES NOT BELONG?

In each row, there are four things that go. One does not belong with the others. Draw a circle around it. Tell why it doesn't belong.

Which things that go can carry more than one person?

SOUNDS OF THINGS THAT GO

Name each vehicle in the picture.
What sound does each vehicle make?

The numbers 1, 2, 3, 4, and 5 are hidden in the picture.
Can you find them all?

YOUR FAVORITE VEHICLE

Draw your favorite vehicle.
Is it big or small?
Is it fast or slow?
What sound does it make?

WHERE WOULD YOU LIKE TO GO?

Draw a picture of the place you would like to go in your favorite vehicle.

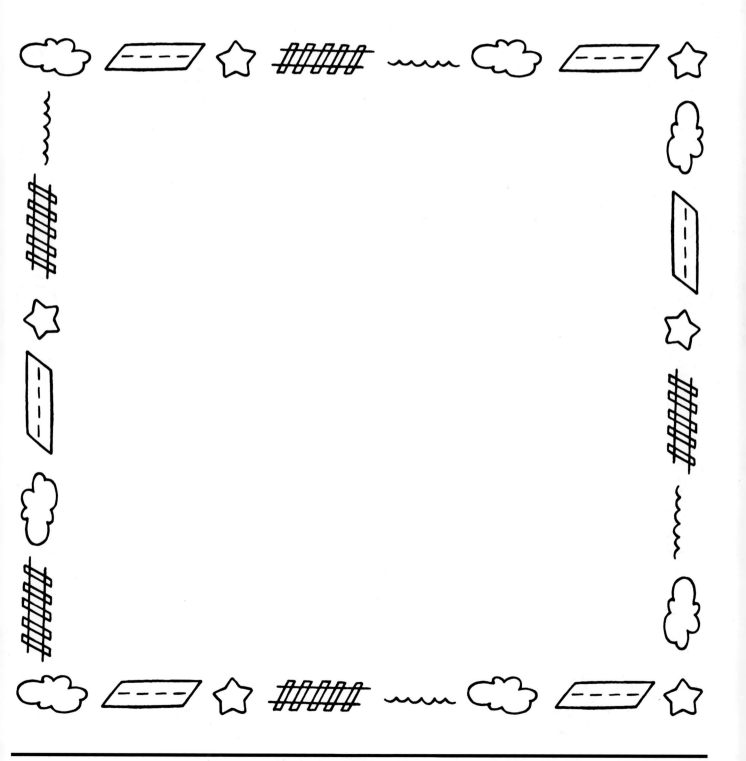

ALL ABOUT THINGS THAT GO

Here's a fun way to find out how much you have learned.
Can you name each vehicle on this page?

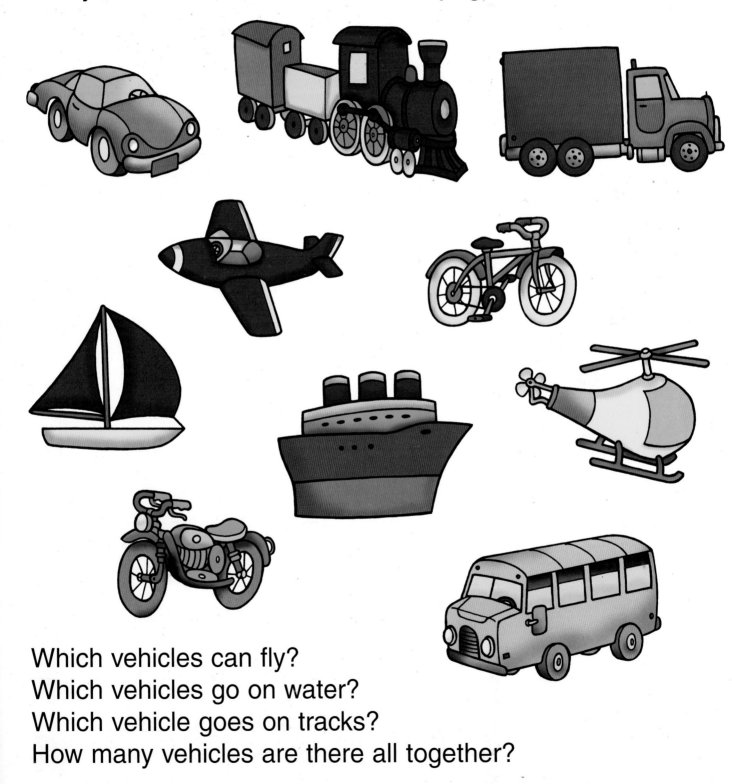

Which vehicles can fly?
Which vehicles go on water?
Which vehicle goes on tracks?
How many vehicles are there all together?